A
the
Nev

BIRDS

ANDREW
CROWE

Illustrated by
DAVE GUNSON

PENGUIN BOOKS

HOW TO USE THIS BOOK

To make it simple to identify an unknown bird, the birds are organised by SIZE (or weight), starting with New Zealand's smallest bird, the **rifleman**. This way, you can go straight to the appropriate section of the book, checking the approximate size of your bird against the page headings, as follows:

It is also important to note WHERE you saw your bird. If you spot a tiny bird in the garden, for example, it is far more likely to be a **warbler** than a **rifleman**. Check the distribution maps too. If you are in the North Island, for example, you can confidently rule out **brown creeper**, **yellowhead**, **little owl** and **kea** (since these are all South Island birds).

An ID checklist helps confirm the bird's identity, beneath which is a clear label to indicate whether or not the bird is unique to New Zealand:

ENDEMIC

Unique to New Zealand – breeds only here.

NATIVE

Found in New Zealand naturally, but breeds in other countries too.

INTRODUCED

Brought to New Zealand by people.

Rifleman / Tītīpounamu

Acanthisitta chloris [Acanthisittidae]

✓ **Seen in old, high-altitude beech forest**
✓ Hops up tree trunks (unlike **grey warbler**, page 4)
✓ Flicks its wings
✓ Call: high-pitched 'zit, zit, zit'

ENDEMIC

New Zealand's smallest bird, the rifleman is usually found only in old, high-altitude beech forest, where it picks insects off the tree trunks. Its call is often too high-pitched for older people to hear. Good spots to find them include Pureora Forest, Pukeiti Rhododendron Reserve near New Plymouth, Lake Rotopounamu, the Waikareiti Track near Lake Waikaremoana, at Day's Bay in Wellington, in the Dunedin Reserves, at Arthur's Pass and in the Eglinton Valley.

Grey Warbler / Riroriro

Gerygone igata [Acanthizidae]

Dark tail feathers with white tips (unlike **rifleman** and **silvereye**)

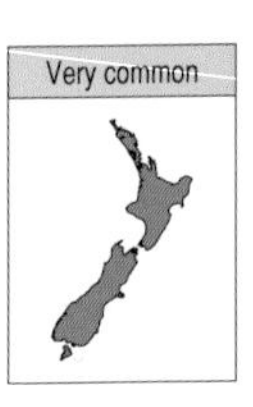

- ✓ In forest, scrub and gardens
- ✓ **Male song: a long warbling trill** (all year, but especially in spring)
- ✓ Heard more often than seen
- ✓ Hovers. Never seems to sit still

ENDEMIC

Found in forest, scrub and gardens, where it eats insects. Often manages to raise just one batch of chicks, before the **shining cuckoo** (page 17) arrives from the Solomon Islands to lay its own eggs in the warbler's nest. At just a few days old, the faster-growing (but still naked) cuckoo chick tips out all the warbler eggs and chicks. In their place, the warbler parents raise a young cuckoo. Although the warbler sings all year, its song is particularly noticeable in spring and summer, thus providing a useful signal to pre-European Māori to start preparing the ground for planting.

Fantail / Pīwakawaka

Rhipidura fuliginosa [Monarchidae]

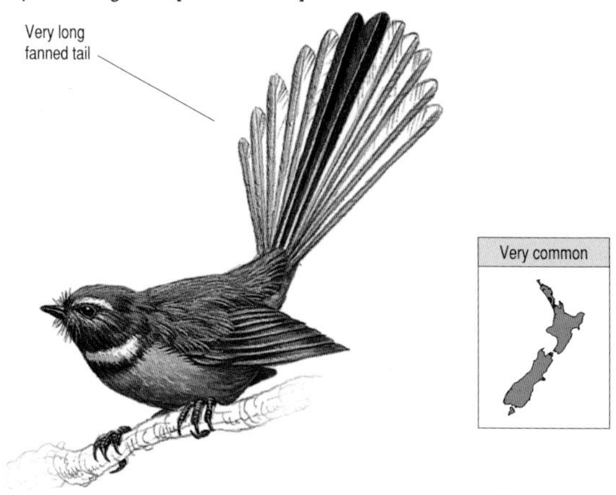

✓ In forest, scrub and gardens
✓ **Friendly. Flits about like a butterfly**
✓ Call: 'cheet, cheet'

NATIVE

Common in forest, scrub and gardens, where it catches flying insects. So bold that it often enters houses in summer and has been known to settle on people's shoulders, their heads or even on an outstretched hand. Other subspecies of the same bird are found in Australia and on some western Pacific Islands.

Tomtit / Miromiro

Petroica macrocephala [Eopsaltriidae]

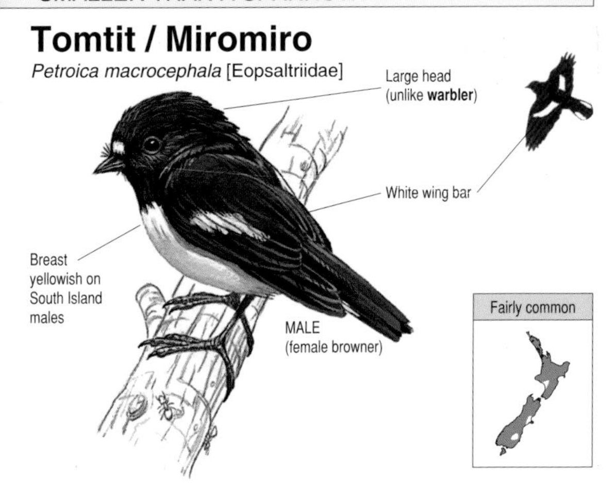

- ✓ Friendly forest bird
- ✓ **Often clings to a tree trunk, flying to the ground to feed**
- ✓ Smaller than **New Zealand robin** (page 22)
- ✓ Male sings a descending warble: 'sweedle-sweedle-sweedle-u-swee'

ENDEMIC

Most commonly seen in mature beech forest, particularly along the western side of the South Island, where it flies from a low perch to the ground to eat insects and worms. They sometimes gather near people in the hope of taking insect food disturbed by a tramper's boot. Particularly good places to find them include Opepe Historic Reserve (near Taupo), Kapiti Island, Arthur's Pass, Eglinton Valley and Stewart Island. Also known as **pied tit** (North Island) or, in the South Island, **ngiru-ngiru** or **yellow-breasted tit**.

Redpoll

Carduelis flammea [Fringillidae]

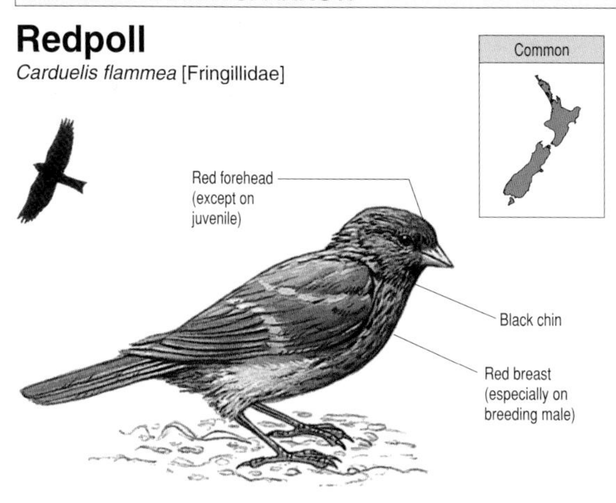

✓ A bird of dry, open country
✓ Noisy flight call: 'chich-chich-chich'
✓ Undulating or circling flight
✓ Feeds on the ground

INTRODUCED

A dull-coloured finch which often goes unnoticed, yet it is common, particularly in high, dry areas of the South Island, but also throughout the country right down to sand dunes at sea level. It eats mainly weed seeds, but also some insects and fruit buds, using its powerful gizzard for breaking up seeds. Plays a useful part in attacking insect pests. In winter, it feeds in flocks of up to 250 birds or more. Nests in low shrubs. Brought here from Europe in the 1860s.

Brown Creeper / Pīpipi

Mohoua novaeseelandiae [Pachycephalidae]

✓ **Not seen in the North Island**
✓ Flocks feed noisily, in forest or scrub
✓ Often spotted near head height, but common among the tree tops
✓ Male song a high-pitched, canary-like 'roh-ree-roh-ree-ree'

ENDEMIC

Lives mostly in forest, sometimes in scrub, where it searches tree trunks for insects. Often forms small, noisy, fast-moving flocks high in the forest canopy. Though hard to see without binoculars, it can sometimes be attracted by squeaking a piece of polystyrene or cork on a wet bottle. In November or December, the **long-tailed cuckoo** (page 36) often lays its egg in the nest, leaving the brown creeper to raise the cuckoo's young. This strange new chick soon comes to dwarf its foster parent, eventually reaching ten times its weight! Good spots to find brown creepers include forest patches on Banks Peninsula, around Dunedin, along the West Coast, Arthur's Pass, Lake Gunn in the Eglinton Valley and Stewart Island.

Silvereye / Tauhou

Zosterops lateralis [Zosteropidae]

✓ In gardens, orchards, scrub and forest
✓ Form flocks in winter, chattering noisily
✓ The bird's song itself is quiet

NATIVE

Also known as **white-eye** or **waxeye**, from its distinctive white eye-ring. Māori named it 'tauhou', meaning 'stranger', for the bird apparently arrived here from Australia as recently as 1832. (It is found also in the south-western Pacific.) It is seen in gardens, orchards, scrub and forest – anywhere where there are trees. Besides nectar and insects, it eats spiders and fruit. To fruit-growers, it can be both helpful and a nuisance, depending on whether it is feeding on insect pests or pecking at fruit. In winter, it is easily attracted to gardens with a piece of apple or a tin of cooking fat on a bird table and also enjoys dipping into bird baths.

Goldfinch

Carduelis carduelis [Fringillidae]

Very common

Bright red face on adults

Bright yellow band on wings

- ✓ In farmland, orchards and gardens
- ✓ Undulating flight, showing flash of gold on wings
- ✓ Male song a twittering 'tsitt-witt-witt' (Sep–Feb)
- ✓ Male and female birds look the same

INTRODUCED

A beautiful and very common finch seen in farmland, orchards and gardens – sometimes on beaches too. The goldfinch eats some insects but mainly uses its powerful gizzard to break up seeds, making it a useful destroyer of weed seeds such as thistle and dandelion. It is often seen in large winter flocks of 50–500 birds, sometimes even with as many as 15,000. With the goldfinch's vibrant colours, it is not surprising that huge numbers were trapped in nineteenth-century England for the cage-bird trade. Brought here from Europe in the 1860s.

Rock Wren / Hurupounamu

Xenicus gilviventris [Acanthisittidae]

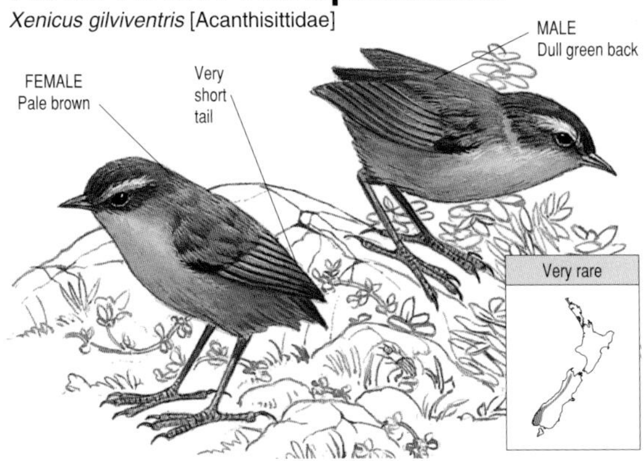

- ✓ **Seen only in the South Island mountains**
- ✓ Bobs up and down on the ground or runs; seldom flies
- ✓ Call: a mouse-like squeak

ENDEMIC

The rock wren lives more like a mouse than a bird, feeding on (or even under) the ground, eating mainly insects and spiders. Most commonly found close to the tree-line, but has been seen as high as 2500 metres above sea level. In winter, it remains in the mountains, hiding in rock crevices beneath the snow or feeding in air spaces between boulders and scrub. The last easily accessible place they could be seen was either side of the Homer Tunnel, near Milford Sound. Listen for a mouse-like squeak coming from amongst a pile of fallen rocks.

Welcome Swallow

Hirundo tahitica [Hirundinidae]

Sleek with pointed wings

Deeply forked tail

Common

✓ Seen over farmland, rivers, wetlands, estuaries and mudflats
✓ **Fly very fast, flitting like a bat**
✓ Often perch on wires, looking like a row of large clothes pegs

NATIVE

Spotted in New Zealand for the first time in 1920, having flown here from Australia. They are more common in the North Island, but are continuing to spread south. Over open water, they snatch small insects or scoop insects from the water surface. They make mud nests which they glue beneath bridges, inside culvert pipes or on cliffs and under the eaves of buildings. In autumn and winter, the birds gather in flocks, many of them migrating to more northern or coastal parts of New Zealand (with some regularly travelling as far afield as Norfolk Island).

Whitehead / Pōpokotea

Mohoua albicilla [Pachycephalidae]

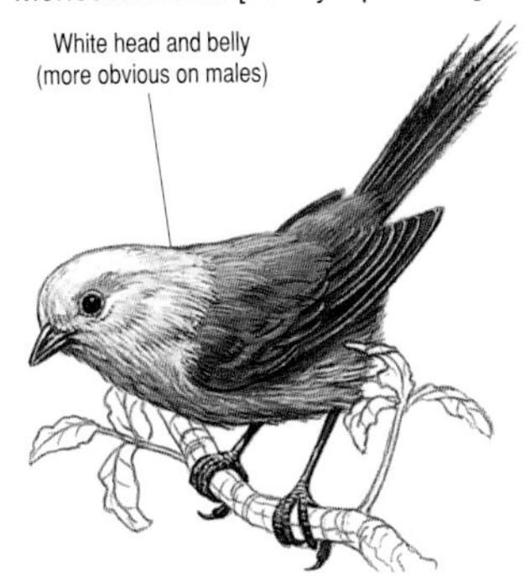

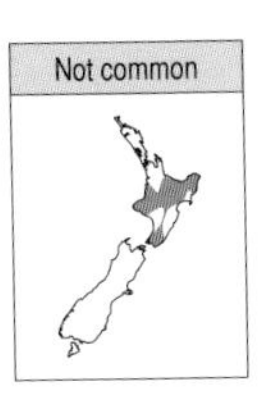

- ✓ **Seen only in North Island forest**
- ✓ Flocks feed noisily, high in the trees
- ✓ Very fast moving
- ✓ Canary-like song: 'swee-swee-swee-chir-chir' (male)

ENDEMIC

In both native forest and mature pine forest, but hard to see without binoculars. Good spots to find them include Tiritiri Matangi Island, the 'Forest Tower' at Pureora Forest, the pine forests of central North Island (e.g. Atiamuri), Opepe Historic Reserve (near Taupo), Lake Rotopounamu, Kapiti Island and Karori Wildlife Sanctuary. It is easily attracted by squeaking a piece of polystyrene or cork on a wet bottle. In November and December, the **long-tailed cuckoo** (page 36) often lays its egg in a whitehead nest, leaving the whitehead to raise a chick which will eventually grow to seven times the weight of its foster parent!

Dunnock (Hedge Sparrow)

Prunella modularis [Prunellidae]

- ✓ Slimmer chest than a **house sparrow** (opposite)
- ✓ **Feeds on bare ground, near hedges or shrubs**
- ✓ Fast warbling song (April–Jan) from a high perch: 'weeso, sissy-weeso, sissy-weeso, sissy-wee' (male)

INTRODUCED

Common among sand dune lupins, along roadsides, in parks, gardens, orchards, scrub and forest. Because of its secretive habits and drab colouring, it is not often noticed and is certainly not well known. Sometimes called the 'hedge sparrow' because it never strays far from hedges or shrubs, and because it looks like a **house sparrow**. It eats insects, spiders and worms (with some fruit and seeds), usually taken from the ground, not far from cover.

House Sparrow / Tiu

Passer domesticus [Ploceidae]

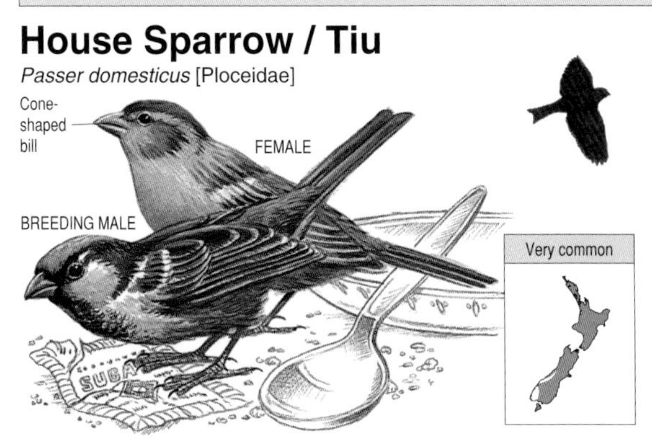

✓ **Most common city bird**
✓ Feeds mainly on the ground
✓ Hops rather than shuffles (unlike **chaffinch**)
✓ Flight: fast and direct

INTRODUCED

Brought here from England in the 1860s to help control insect pests in crops. Unfortunately, the sparrow eats far more seeds than insects, so soon became New Zealand's greatest bird pest for farmers. In towns, it has learnt to trigger the electronic sensors of automatic sliding doors to reach café crumbs, flying into warehouses, supermarkets and hospitals too, to find human-produced food, such as bread, sugar and fat. It is also common on beaches, especially among sand dunes. One of the easiest birds to attract to the garden with a bird bath or with crumbs left on a bird table. At dusk, large groups are often heard chattering from nests in dense trees or hedges, particularly in bamboo or tall conifer trees. Now found over two-thirds of the world's land surface.

Chaffinch / Pahirini

Fringilla coelebs [Fringillidae]

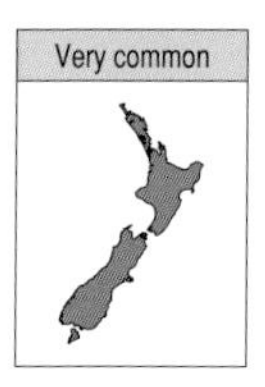

- ✓ In parks, gardens, farmland, scrub, forest and above the tree-line
- ✓ Shuffles (rather than walks or hops)
- ✓ Undulating flight showing white wingbar and outer tail feathers
- ✓ Male song from high perch (July–Jan): 'chip chip chip tell tell tell cherry-erry-erry tissi **cheweeo**'

INTRODUCED

Common throughout the country – not only in parks, gardens, farmland and scrub, but also deep inside native and exotic forest; sometimes even in the mountains, above the tree-line. Indeed, there is nowhere too remote for them. They are encouraged into parks and gardens to take crumbs from bird tables and picnickers. In autumn and winter, they form flocks of several hundred birds.

Shining Cuckoo / Pīpīwharauroa

Chrysococcyx lucidus [Cuculidae]

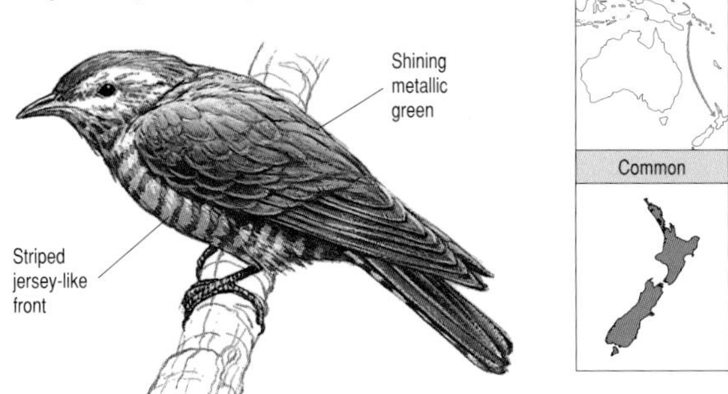

✓ In forest, scrub and gardens
✓ Usually heard rather than seen
✓ Song: 'tu**wee** tu**wee** tu**wee** tu**wee** ti**woo**' (spring and summer)

NATIVE

Although this cuckoo lives in forest, scrub and gardens, it is rarely seen because its green colouring makes such good camouflage. The easiest place to spot them is in farm willow trees or gum trees, or when one stuns itself by flying into a window. It spends the winter in Papua New Guinea, Indonesia and the Solomon Islands, heading south to New Zealand in late September and early October to lay its eggs in the nest of a **grey warbler**, leaving that bird to raise its young. At the end of summer, the shining cuckoo heads back north again. On its return to New Zealand, it often comes back to the same spot where it was born. Also found in Australia, Vanuatu and New Caledonia. It feeds on insects, particularly caterpillars.

Yellowhead / Mohua

Mohoua ochrocephala [Pachycephalidae]

✓ **Seen only in mature South Island forest**
✓ Unlike the common **yellowhammer** (opposite), it is never found in open country
✓ Flocks feed noisily high in the trees (except in spring to early summer)
✓ Canary-like song, with buzzes (male)

ENDEMIC

This rare and attractive bird is found only in the South Island, in mature native forest, especially beech. A good place to see them is in the roadside forests of the Eglinton Valley, Lake Gunn Track and at Haast Pass. From mid-summer to the end of winter, they gather into flocks of up to 25 birds roaming the tree tops, often along with other species of forest birds. It can be very hard to see without binoculars, but can be attracted by squeaking a piece of polystyrene on a glass bottle. Feeds on insects and spiders. Nests in holes in old trees. Sometimes, the **long-tailed cuckoo** (page 36) uses these to lays its own eggs, leaving the yellowhead to raise its young. Also known as **bush canary**.

Yellowhammer

Emberiza citrinella [Emberizidae]

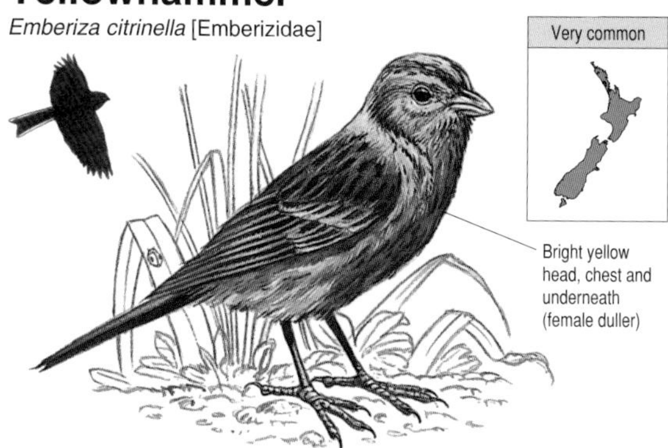

- ✓ In rough open country and orchards
- ✓ Feeds mainly on the ground, hopping
- ✓ Flight often undulating, showing white outer tail feathers
- ✓ Sings from perch (Aug–Feb): 'a little bit of bread and no cheese' (male)

INTRODUCED

This finch-like bird was brought here in the 1860s from Europe and is probably now more common here than in England. It is found mostly in rough open country and orchards from sea level to subalpine tussock, but is uncommon in built-up areas. In winter and spring, they can gather in large flocks of up to 200–300 birds. It eats seeds, insects and spiders and builds a rough nest on, or near, the ground. A less colourful relative, the **cirl bunting**, is sometimes seen in the north and east of the South Island.

Greenfinch

Carduelis chloris [Fringillidae]

Common

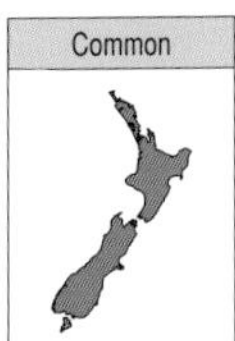

- ✓ In hedges, orchards and edges of pine forest
- ✓ Male song (Aug–Feb) from high perch in descending notes: 'chichichi tu zweet zweet zweet' or a jeering 'dzwee'
- ✓ Undulating flight, showing yellow on tail and wings

INTRODUCED

Brought here from Europe in the 1860s and now common in larger gardens, hedged farmland, orchards and the edges of pine forest. Can be attracted into gardens with a bird table. Its main food is seeds, but it eats fruit buds too and some insects, which it will happily pick out of car radiators. In winter and spring, large flocks can be seen among farm weeds.

Bellbird / Korimako

Anthornis melanura [Meliphagidae]

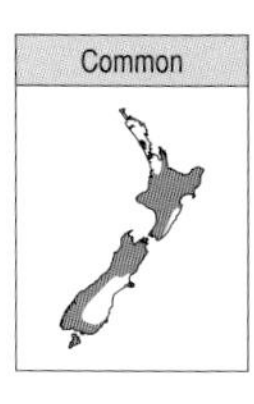

- ✓ In forest, scrub and gardens
- ✓ **Song: bell-like (with no grunts, coughs or chortles)**
- ✓ Rare in Waikato and Northland
- ✓ Fast, noisy, whirring flight

ENDEMIC

The song of korimako – at dawn and dusk – can often sound like ringing bells or like flutes playing. Unlike European songbirds, both male and female birds sing and do so throughout the year. Māori hunted them, using a 'call-leaf' to attract the bird, placing a flat or doubled leaf between their lips and sucking air to make a chirping sound. Found mostly in forest, but sometimes in scrub and gardens, especially in the South Island. Feeds on nectar, honeydew, insects and fruit, making it an important pollinator of native forest flowers and carrier of small seeds.

New Zealand Robin / Toutouwai

Petroica australis [Eopsaltriidae]

- ✓ **Hops about on the forest floor**
- ✓ Friendly and curious
- ✓ Call: a soft 'tok, tok, tok'
- ✓ Song: 'tweep-tweep-tweep-too-too-too' (male)

ENDEMIC

Often perches on a low branch or tree trunk, flying to the forest floor to catch insects and worms. Will sometimes land on people's heads or boots or feed from their hands. Found among old trees in both native and pine forests. Good spots to see them include Tiritiri Matangi Island, forests around the Rotorua Lakes and Taupo, Kapiti Island, Karori Wildlife Sanctuary, Arthur's Pass and in the Eglinton Valley. The famous **black robin** of the Chatham Islands, rescued from the brink of extinction in the 1980s, looks similar, but is a different species.

Stitchbird / Hihi

Notiomystis cincta [Meliphagidae]

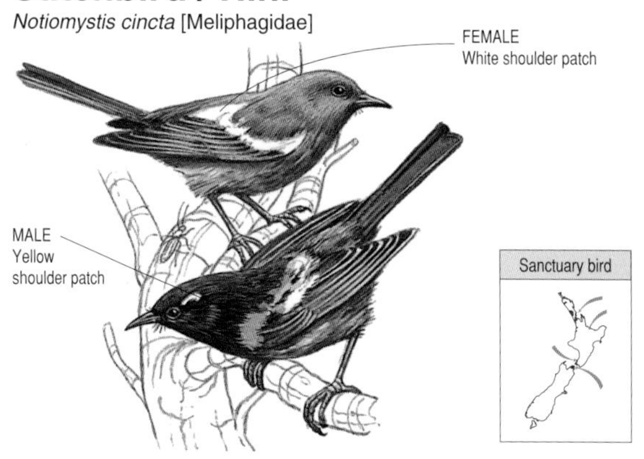

- ✓ **Seen only on a few small island sanctuaries**
- ✓ Often seen in pairs
- ✓ Call: 'stit-stit-stit' or 'stitch'

ENDEMIC

Once common in the North Island but now survives only on a few small islands, like Tiritiri Matangi, Little Barrier and Kapiti Islands, and on Mokoia Island in Lake Rotorua. Can now be seen at Karori Wildlife Sanctuary too, possibly now even in the Waitakere Ranges! The stitchbird eats nectar, fruit and some insects, often feeding near the ground. Flax flowers are a favourite. Like the **bellbird** and **tūī**, it is a 'honeyeater' with a brush-tipped tongue and, like those birds, it plays an important role in pollinating native forest flowers and carrying smaller seeds. Unlike most other honeyeaters, though, it nests in holes in the trunks of trees.

Fernbird / Mātātā

Bowdleria punctata [Sylviidae]

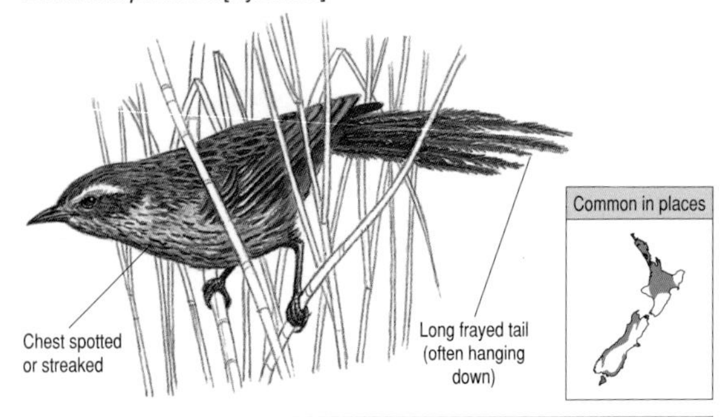

✓ **Well-hidden in low scrub, usually near swamps**
✓ Slips between low branches like a mouse, rarely flying far
✓ Heard more often than seen
✓ Call: 'utik' (usually heard in spring)

ENDEMIC

The fernbird stays well hidden in low scrub, usually near freshwater and tidal swamps (but can also sometimes be found well away from water in low scrub and bracken). It slips through the low tangle of branches like a mouse, searching for insects and spiders. A good place to see fernbirds is actually named after them: Mātātā Lagoons, west of Whakatane. The trick to finding them is to listen for their main call: 'utik', a sound which is usually produced by a pair of birds, one calling the 'uu' part, the other answering 'tik'. Easily attracted by making simple squeaks, either by rubbing a piece of cork or polystyrene on wet glass, or simply by sucking air between your teeth. Early settlers called it **swamp-sparrow**.

Skylark

Alauda arvensis [Alaudidae]

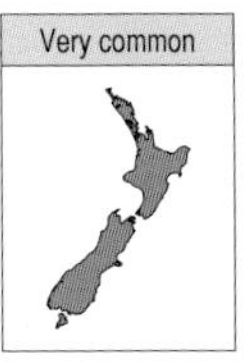

✓ In sand dunes and farmland to subalpine tussock
✓ **Male sings non-stop while hovering high overhead (unlike pipit)**
✓ Feeds on the ground

INTRODUCED

European settlers brought this bird here in the 1860s for its warbling flight song. It is now far more common here than in England. Usually noticed in spring, singing non-stop while hovering high overhead, sometimes for as long as 20 minutes at a stretch. It sings while rising almost vertically until it is almost out of sight, and continues to sing as it drops back down to the ground. Very common in open country from coastal sand dunes and farmland to subalpine tussock, nesting and feeding on the ground, eating mainly seeds, with some insects and spiders.

New Zealand Pipit / Pīhoihoi

Anthus novaeseelandiae [Motacillidae]

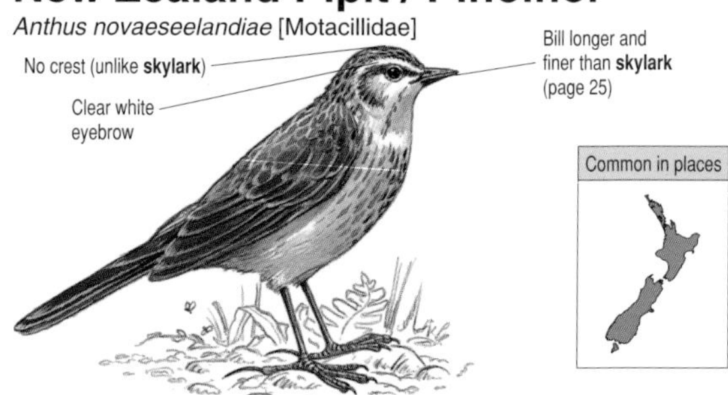

- ✓ On beaches, rough pasture and above the tree-line
- ✓ **Runs a short distance, stops and flicks its tail** (unlike **skylark** – previous page)
- ✓ Feeds mostly on the ground
- ✓ Makes short, fast swoops (unlike **skylark**)
- ✓ Calls from low perch: 'pi-pit'

INTRODUCED

On beaches, the pipit has the odd habit of running and stopping, then flicking its tail up and down. Also seen hopping up coastal cliffs, in rough pasture, along shingle riverbeds, gravel roads, scrubby roadsides and way up into the mountains – even above the tree-line. Eats insects, spiders and sandhoppers, also some seeds, feeding mostly on the ground. Builds its nest on the ground too. Although found naturally in many other countries (where it is known as **Richard's pipit**), the four subspecies here are found only in New Zealand. Previously known as the **ground lark** because of its lark-like looks and habit of staying close to the ground (even though larks and pipits are not closely related).

Yellow-Crowned Parakeet / Kākāriki

Cyanoramphus auriceps [Psittacidae]

✓ **Seen only in mature forest, mostly in the tree tops**
✓ Half the weight of a **rosella** (page 33)
✓ High-pitched cry: 'kita-kita-kita-kita'

ENDEMIC

Only in mature native forest, usually high up in the trees, where they nest in holes in old trees. Most common in South Island beech forests. Other good spots to see them include the forest tower at Pureora Forest, the Eglinton Valley and nearby Rees, Dart and Routeburn Tracks and on Stewart Island. An **orange-fronted** form is sometimes seen in North Canterbury and a similar subspecies is found on the Chatham Islands. The slightly larger **red-crowned parakeet** (*C. novaezelandiae*) is rare on the main islands but can be seen on Tiritiri Matangi, Kapiti and Stewart Islands.

Kingfisher / Kōtare

*Todiramphus sanctus** [Alcedinidae]

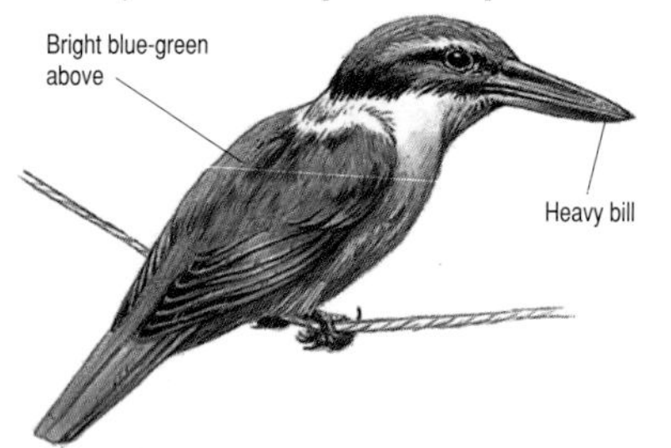

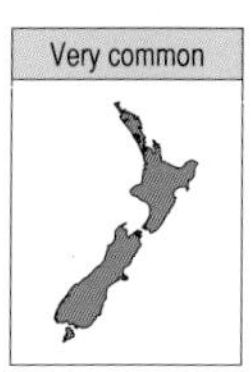

- ✓ On shores of estuaries, farmland, near rivers or lakes, also in forest
- ✓ Often perches on wires, branches, rocks or fenceposts
- ✓ Direct, arrow-like flight
- ✓ **Call: a loud 'weet-weet-weet-weet'**

NATIVE

New Zealand's only native kingfisher. More common in the North Island, often along the shores of estuaries, but also in farmland, near rivers or lakes, sometimes on sandy beaches along the high tide line or on rocky shores. It is common in forest too, where it is heard but usually too high in the trees to be seen. In winter, it moves down to the coast, often perching on a look-out post, branch, rock or wire. From here, it dives for its prey without landing. The kingfisher hunts small crabs, large insects, spiders, earthworms, lizards, mice, tadpoles, small fish, freshwater crayfish and small birds. Its nest is a small tunnel in a clay bank or a hole in a rotting tree. Other subspecies of the same kingfisher are native to Australia and New Caledonia.

* Previously *Halcyon sancta*

Song Thrush

Turdus philomelos [Muscicapidae]

- ✓ In gardens, parks, orchards, farm hedges, forests and scrub
- ✓ Feeds mostly on the ground (**hopping**)
- ✓ Male sings from high perch, **repeated phrases**: 'Did you do it? Did you do it? I saw you. I saw you. . .' (May–Dec)
- ✓ Male and female birds look the same

INTRODUCED

Very common in gardens, parks, orchards, farm hedges, forests and scrub, right up to subalpine altitudes. The song thrush runs or hops a few steps, then stops with its head cocked, as if listening for worms to pull from the ground. But the bird is not listening; it is tilting its head to get a better view. When eating snails, it often carries them to a special stone on which to smash the shells open. But, apart from eating common garden snails, it also eats rare native land snails, insects, spiders, millipedes, hoppers and some fruit.

Saddleback / Tīeke

Philesturnus carunculatus [Callaeidae]

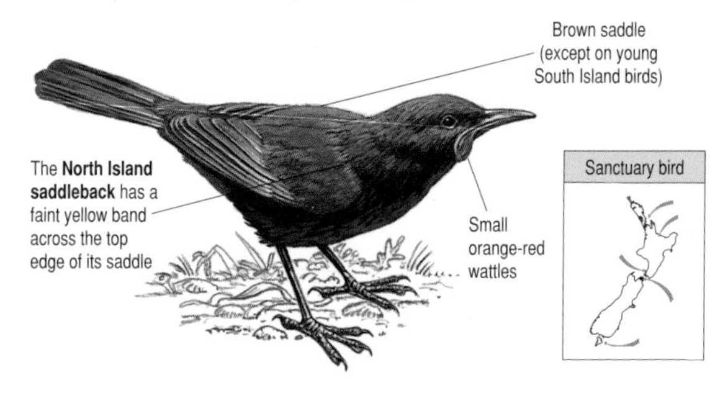

- ✓ **Seen only in sanctuaries and offshore islands**
- ✓ Stays mostly on or near the ground
- ✓ Short flights; hops between branches or runs up branches
- ✓ Main call: a loud 'ke-eet, te-te-te-te'

ENDEMIC

Two subspecies, one on offshore islands around the North Island, and a much rarer subspecies on islands off the South Island. This South Island bird is one of the first birds in the world to be saved from extinction by people. Today, saddlebacks can be most easily seen on Tiritiri Matangi and Little Barrier Islands, Mokoia Island in Lake Rotorua, on Kapiti and Motuara Islands and in Karori Wildlife Sanctuary. It usually nests near the ground, often in holes in trees, where it lays two or three eggs. The saddleback eats insects and berries – often from the forest floor – using its strong, chisel-shaped bill to dig into rotting logs. Like the **kōkako** and extinct **huia**, it belongs to the wattlebird family – a family with no close relatives anywhere else in the world.

Myna

Acridotheres tristis [Sturnidae]

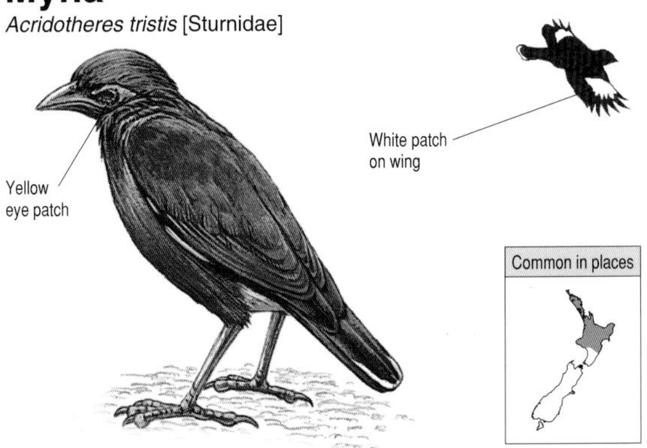

- ✓ **Seen only in the North Island – often on roads**
- ✓ Takes waddling jerky steps
- ✓ Song: raucous with bell-like notes (all year)
- ✓ Call: 'a**chu**kee a**chu**kee a**chu**kee'

INTRODUCED

Often seen on sealed roads in the northern North Island, picking up insects killed by cars. Also common in towns, gardens, farmland, orchards and on the coast, where they can destroy the eggs and chicks of native birds, often forcing the parent bird to abandon its nest. It makes its own nests in holes – often in trees, but also in cliffs and buildings. Good at copying the sound of doorbells or cell phones. Originally from Afghanistan and India. Introduced to New Zealand in the 1870s, originally to the South Island where they have since died out.

Long-Tailed Cuckoo / Koekoeā

Eudynamys taitensis [Cuculidae]

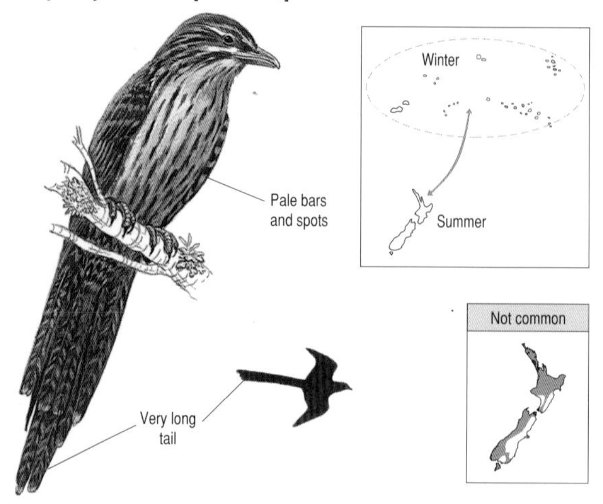

✓ **In the tree tops of tall forests**
✓ Piercing screech late spring to summer: 'zzwhoo**eesht**' (even at night)

ENDEMIC

Breeds only in New Zealand, but spends winter in the tropical Pacific, returning in early October to lay its eggs in the nests of **whitehead**, **brown creeper** or **yellowhead**. By early March most birds have left again. Good spots to find them include forested stretches of the Wanganui River, tall forests in central North Island and Westland, Kapiti Island, Eglinton Valley and Stewart Island.

Morepork / Ruru

Ninox novaeseelandiae [Strigidae]

✓ In forest, scrub and gardens
✓ **Heard at night; seldom seen** (except when hunting near lights)
✓ Call: **'more pork'**, a screeching **'krree'** or hooting calls

NATIVE

Fairly common in forest, scrub and gardens, though not often seen, as it sleeps during the day on a well-hidden branch, in a hole – or fork – of a tree. At late dusk, it is sometimes seen around outdoor lights, even in large cities like Auckland, where it swoops for large moths and flying beetles. Also hunts small birds, mice, rats and lizards. Its silent flight is due to soft feathers along the edges of its wings. It has exceptional hearing too, due partly to the disks around its eyes which channel sound to its large ears. Europeans called it 'morepork' in imitation of its call. A similar subspecies is found on Norfolk Island.

Little Owl

Athene noctua [Strigidae]

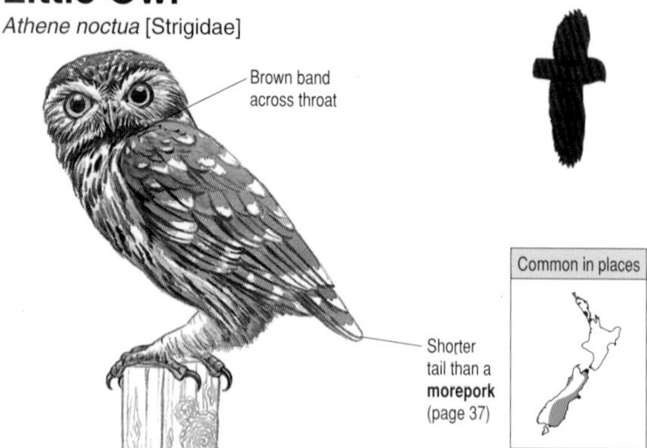

✓ **Seen only in the South Island** (mostly east coast)
✓ **Hunts by day** (unlike the native **morepork** owl)
✓ Flight silent and 'bouncing'
✓ Call: a high-pitched 'kiew'

INTRODUCED

This owl was brought here from Germany in 1906 to help control **sparrows** and **finches**. Unfortunately, however, its main food is insects, spiders and earthworms. It also hunts – both by day and by night – along roadsides for mice, rabbits, frogs and lizards, often walking on the ground or running after its food. It lives in hedges, hay barns and clumps of trees (but only in the South Island). Unlike the native **morepork**, it is often seen perching in the open in late afternoon, sunning itself on a fencepost. Also known as the **German owl**, but is found naturally in other parts of Europe too, in northern Africa and western Asia.

California Quail

Callipepla californica [Phasianidae]

✓ In open, low scrub, roadsides and riverbeds
✓ **Male call: 'macwerta, macwerta'**
✓ Runs, taking off with a loud whirr of wings, calling: **'tek tek tek'**
✓ Sometimes perches in trees too

INTRODUCED

Introduced from the western United States in the 1860s, the California quail lives in open country with low scrub, commonly feeding along roadsides and riverbeds. It feeds on fallen seeds, leaves and a few small insects, but runs or flies for cover when disturbed. It nests in well-hidden spots on the ground, laying up to 22 eggs at a time, many of which get eaten by hedgehogs. In autumn, the large families sometimes join up to make even larger groups of up to 50 birds. In Northland, the smaller Australian **brown quail** (with no topknot) is also common.

Kōkako

Callaeas cinerea [Callaeidae]

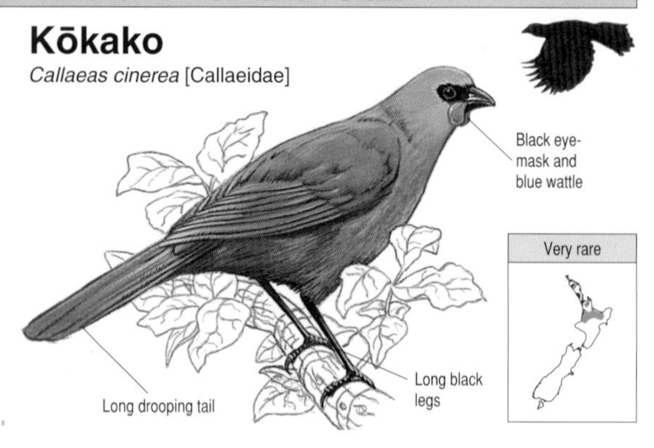

- ✓ **Not seen in the South Island or Stewart Island**
- ✓ Runs or leaps about in the tree tops of tall native forest
- ✓ Heard mostly at dawn (rarely seen)
- ✓ Song: loud, sad organ-like notes
- ✓ Twice the weight of a **tūī** (page 34)

ENDEMIC

Now so rare in the wild, that you are unlikely to come across kōkako by chance. It lives in tall native forest, often staying high up in the trees, where it eats berries, leaves, fern fronds, flowers, buds and insects. Here, it balances on one leg like a parrot, eating food held by the other foot. Although it has very small wings and rarely flies far, it will glide or use its very long legs to leap between branches or run like a squirrel. Its best chance for survival these days is on off-shore islands and 'mainland islands', where rats, possums and stoats are excluded or heavily controlled. An excellent place to see them in the wild is Tiritiri Matangi Island, near Auckland.

Spur-Winged Plover

Vanellus miles [Charadriidae]

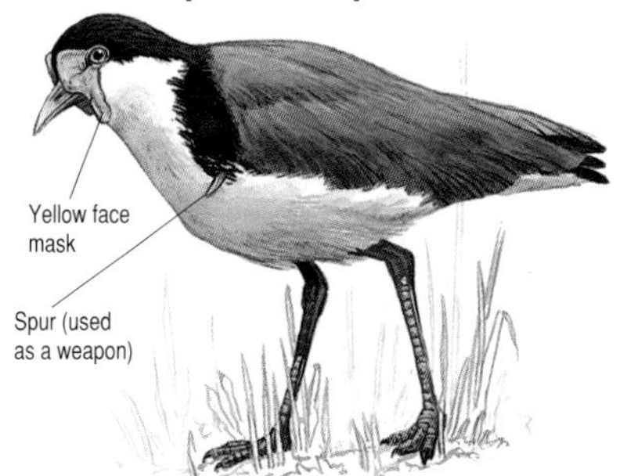

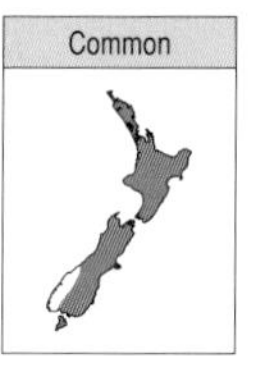

- ✓ On farmland, estuaries, riverbeds and beaches
- ✓ Call: **'kitter kitter kitter'** (day or night)
- ✓ Runs and stops when feeding
- ✓ In flight: slow wingbeats

NATIVE

Pronounced 'pluvver'. The odd bird began arriving here from Australia in the 1800s, but they did not begin breeding here until 1932. They have since spread throughout New Zealand, but remain more common in the South Island. Having made this journey without human help, it is regarded as native to New Zealand (or 'self-introduced'). It helps farmers by eating grass grubs and harmful caterpillars, but also eats earthworms, seeds and leaves. It can be aggressive towards other birds, often screaming and dive-bombing them, striking out with its wings or sharp wing-spurs. It will chase people away from its nest too; if necessary, attacking with its wing-spurs which are long enough to penetrate clothing. Known in Australia as **masked lapwing**.

Australian Magpie / Makipae

Gymnorhina tibicen [Cracticidae]

- ✓ In farm trees, along roadsides and in cities, also mature forest
- ✓ Loud, flute-like song: 'quardle oodle ardle wardle doodle' (all year)
- ✓ Direct flight; rapid wingbeats

INTRODUCED

Introduced from Australia in the 1860s to help control insect pests. It can be fiercely territorial, attacking native birds, so is now often trapped. It will even dive-bomb people and other large animals coming near its nest, swooping from behind and sometimes striking with its claws. Its food includes seeds, spiders, worms, snails, lizards, mice, and dead or dying sheep. Very common in open farmland with pine, macrocarpa, willow or gum trees, but also along roadsides and in cities, sometimes even in mature forest. It usually builds its nest in a tree. Two subspecies seen here – the **white-backed magpie** and the less common **black-backed magpie** – both interbreed. Although named after the **magpie** of Europe, the two birds are not closely related. Australian settlers found the link only in the similarity of the bird's black and white colouring.

Rock Pigeon (City Pigeon)

Columba livia [Columbidae]

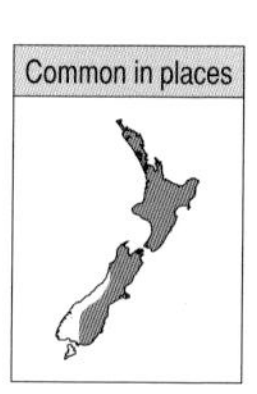

✓ In city parks, on ledges of city buildings and sea cliffs
✓ Smaller than the native **New Zealand pigeon** (page 47)
✓ Call: 'oor-roo-cooo'

INTRODUCED

This is the tame pigeon seen in city parks or nesting on the ledges of city buildings, but it is also found here in its natural habitat, along sea cliffs. Introduced from Europe. In towns, it eats mainly food scraps, but in country areas it can be a nuisance in newly sown pea and bean crops. The chicks are fed at first on a regurgitated cheesy substance called 'pigeon milk' which comes from inside the throat of its parents. Also known as **feral pigeon.** City birds can be any shade from white to dark grey (or a mixture of these colours). The related pale brown **spotted dove** of Asia (with chequerboard spots on its neck) is occasionally seen or heard in Auckland gardens, as is the rarer cream-coloured **Barbary dove** from north Africa and the Middle East.

Rook

Corvus frugilegus [Corvidae]

- ✓ Common only in farmland around Hawke's Bay and Banks Peninsula
- ✓ Bigger than an **Australian magpie** (page 42)
- ✓ Calls: 'caw', 'kah' or 'kiow'
- ✓ In flight: broad 'fingered' wingtips

INTRODUCED

Common only in farmland around Hawke's Bay and on Banks Peninsula, near Christchurch, where it nests in the tops of tall pine trees, macrocarpas and gums. Brought here from England in the 1860s to help control insect pests such as grass grubs. Unfortunately for farmers, it also feeds on newly sown seed, often working its way along a row, pulling them out, one by one. Shooting and poisoning in Hawke's Bay in the 1960s and 1970s did reduce their numbers but also displaced many birds so that the rook population is now spread over a larger area. They nest in large colonies and gather in winter into larger flocks to roost.

New Zealand Falcon / Kārearea

Falco novaeseelandiae [Falconidae]

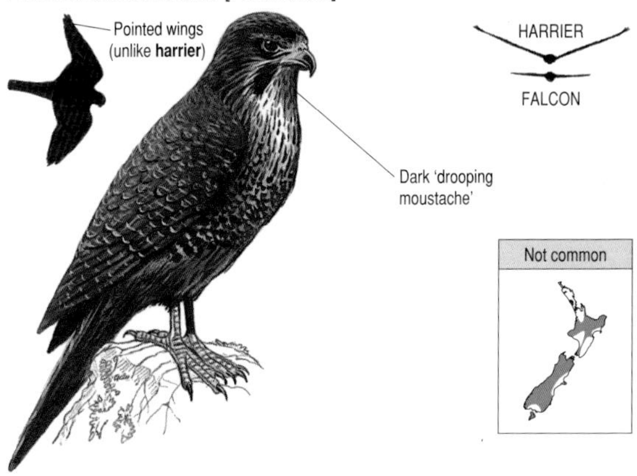

- ✓ In forest and tussockland; also high country farmland
- ✓ Half the size (or weight) of a **harrier** (page 48)
- ✓ Swoops from perch; seldom hovers
- ✓ Flies like a **pigeon** with fast wingbeats
- ✓ Shrill scream: **'keek-keek-keek-keek'**

ENDEMIC

Mainly in forest and tussockland, but also in rough, high country farmland on the eastern side of the South Island. A formidable hunter of other birds, lizards, young rabbits and hares. In an attacking dive, it can reach speeds of up to 180 km/hr. Nests on cliff ledges and among perching lilies, high in the forks of trees.

Kākā

Nestor meridionalis [Psittacidae]

Red underwings

Not common

- ✓ Usually found in (or flying over) forest
- ✓ Noisy call: **'kra, kra, ka'** (day or night) and liquid whistling song
- ✓ Listen for falling bark and broken sticks
- ✓ Flight quieter and slower than a **New Zealand pigeon** (opposite)

ENDEMIC

Seen in mature native forest, particularly along the West Coast of the South Island, although the odd bird is seen in central Auckland. Easy places to see them include the forest tower at Pureora Forest, Kapiti Island, Karori Wildlife Sanctuary, Eglinton Valley and Stewart Island. They behave like monkeys, using their bills or feet to climb or swing through the branches, feeding day and night, using their hooked bills to tear off loose bark and rotten wood to get at grubs.

New Zealand Pigeon / Kererū

Hemiphaga novaeseelandiae [Columbidae]

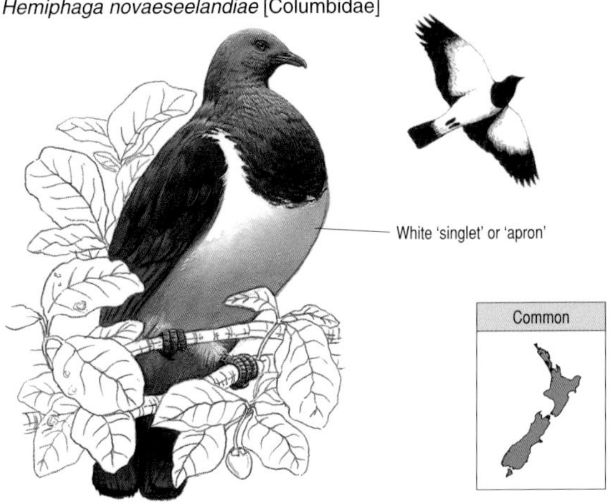

- ✓ In or over native forest; sometimes in gardens
- ✓ **Heavy flight with slow, whooshing wingbeats, crashing clumsily through the branches**
- ✓ Makes spectacular stall dives in spring

ENDEMIC

Lives mostly in native forest, but in winter will sometimes feed in gardens. Can swallow whole seeds of miro, mataī, tawa, taraire, pūriri and karaka; indeed, these trees are entirely dependant on this bird for the dispersal of their seeds. Other Māori names include **kūkū**, **kūkupa** (Northland), **parea** (Chatham Islands). Also known as **wood pigeon**.

Australasian Harrier / Kāhu

Circus approximans [Accipitridae]

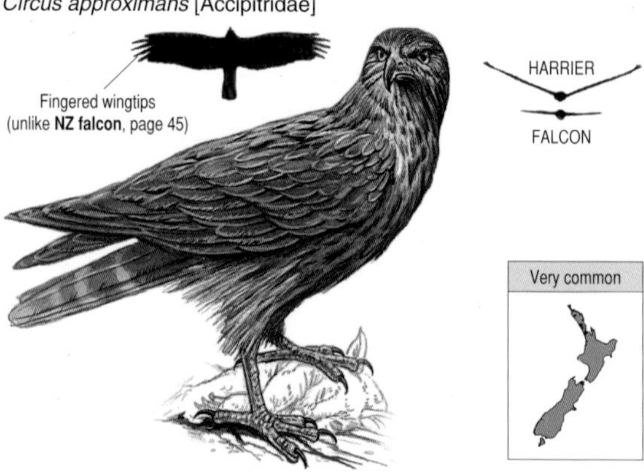

- ✓ Often seen in the middle of the road, or circling overhead
- ✓ Twice the size of a **New Zealand falcon** (page 45)
- ✓ Slow wingbeats (unlike a **New Zealand falcon**)
- ✓ Young birds are darker coloured

NATIVE

Often seen in the middle of the road, feeding on dead possums and hedgehogs hit by cars. It hunts by day, using its sharp claws rather than its bill to catch its food, which includes rabbits, hares, rats, mice, small birds, lizards, frogs, fish and crickets. The harrier circles for hours over farmland, scrub or forest, swamps, riverbeds or sand dunes. The same bird is also found in Australia, New Guinea and several Pacific Islands.

Kea

Nestor notabilis [Psittacidae]

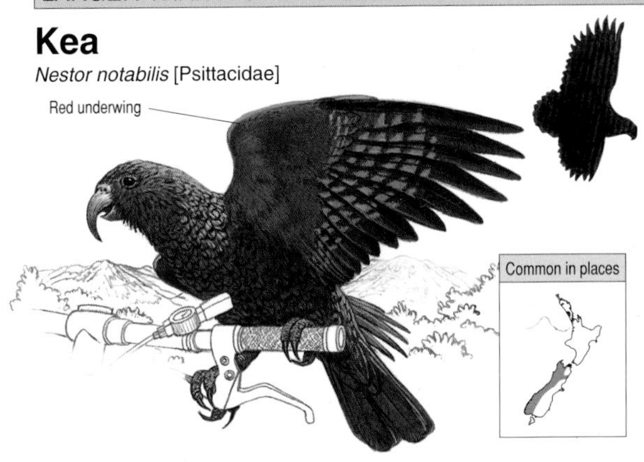

- ✓ **Seen only in the South Island, mostly in the mountains**
- ✓ Screeching call while flying: 'ke-e-e-e-a'
- ✓ Aerobatic flight and cheeky

ENDEMIC

One of the world's few alpine parrots, the kea lives only in the South Island – mainly in the mountains. Surprisingly, it nests in burrows in high altitude forest and scrub. It is often first noticed in skifields or alpine carparks but, on the western side of the Southern Alps, it comes right down into low-lying flat country. It eats mostly fruit, seeds, leaves and buds, but also insects, bird chicks and dead animals. Has the comical habit of sliding down the roofs of tents, tramping huts or windscreens of parked cars, or even perching on the glass edge of half-open car windows. Nuisance birds are sometimes caught and kept as caged pets.

Pūkeko

Porphyrio porphyrio [Rallidae]

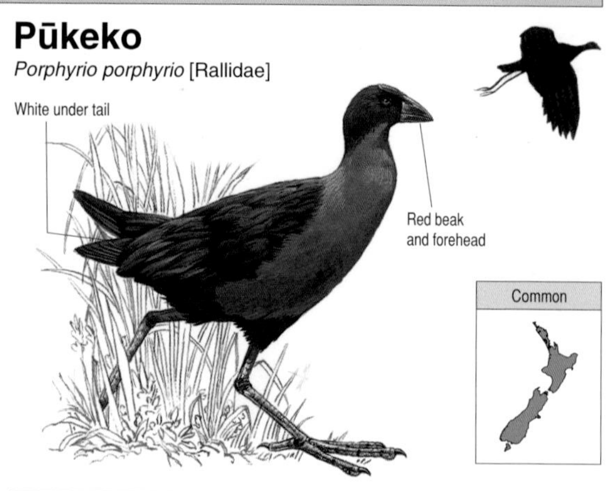

- ✓ In swamps, open farmland, along roadsides and motorway verges
- ✓ Call: a loud screech (day or night)
- ✓ Sometimes perches in trees
- ✓ Flies with fast wingbeats, legs dangling

NATIVE

This swamp bird is often seen grazing in open farmland, along roadsides and motorway verges. Unafraid of cars, it is often hit. Also found from southern Europe and Africa, through Asia to Australia and the western Pacific where it is known as the **purple swamphen**. Closely related to the **takahē** (page 55). It eats leaves, worms, insects, spiders, frogs and the chicks and eggs of ground-nesting birds. Although it doesn't usually travel far, one bird, which was moved 96 km, found its own way home in eight days. Another banded bird travelled 240 km.

Pheasant / Peihana

Phasianus colchicus [Phasianidae]

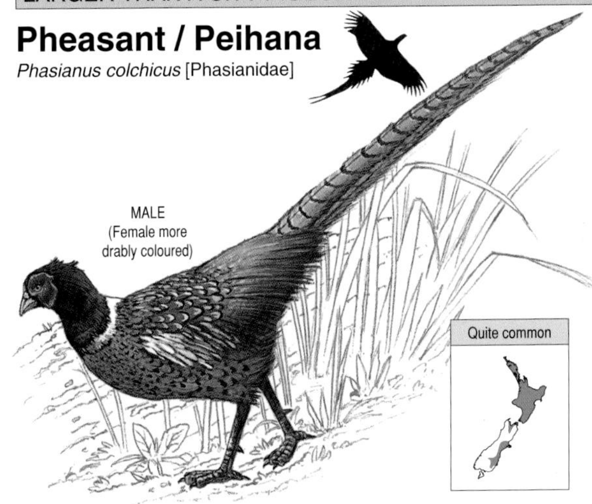

- ✓ **Seen mostly in the North Island**
- ✓ On quiet roadsides, scrub edges, riverbanks and sand dunes
- ✓ Bursts noisily into flight with whirring wingbeats, then glides to the ground
- ✓ Very loud male call: 'kok **kok**'

INTRODUCED

Introduced to New Zealand for sport in the 1840s. Now common in the north and west of the North Island, along back country roadsides, scrubby edges of farmland, riverbanks and in sand dunes, where they use hedges or corridors of scrub as cover when travelling from one area to another. They feed and nest on the ground, eating leaves, seeds, berries and insects. Also known as **ring-necked pheasant**.

Weka

Gallirallus australis [Rallidae]

- ✓ Mostly in forest and scrub. **Rare in the North Island**
- ✓ Runs fast with neck outstretched, or strides along with tail flicking
- ✓ Call: a series of rising 'coo**eets**' (day or night)
- ✓ Cannot fly

ENDEMIC

Although the weka does have wings, it cannot fly. It is commonly mistaken for a **kiwi**, but weka are much easier to see than kiwi since they are often active during the day. On the South Island West Coast, they even gather around some roadside picnic sites. It lives mostly in forest and scrub, eating a huge range of foods including eggs, rats, small birds, lizards, worms, snails, insects, seeds and fruit. For this reason, they often need to be kept away from other endangered wildlife. Easy places to see them include Kawau, Kapiti and Stewart Islands, Karori Wildlife Sanctuary and north-west South Island.

Brown Kiwi / Kiwi

Apteryx australis [Apterygidae]

- ✓ In forest, scrub and tussock
- ✓ **Active only at night** (except on Stewart Island)
- ✓ Calls at night: 'kiw**eee**' 10–25 times, each call rising in pitch
- ✓ Snuffles at night like a hedgehog
- ✓ Cannot fly (has no wings)

ENDEMIC

Kiwi are increasingly rare – largely because of dogs, but also because of stoats, rats, ferrets, pigs, wild cats and possums. By far the easiest place to see one is in one of the special kiwi houses. There are at least four species (**brown kiwi**, **tokoeka**, **great spotted kiwi** and **little spotted kiwi**). The kiwi shown is the most common of these. It comes out from its burrow at night in forest, scrub and tussock and eats mostly worms, but also insects and fallen fruit. The bird's loud night call is usually heard about 40 minutes after sunset. One of the best places to see and hear wild kiwi is at Mason Bay on Stewart Island where **tokoeka kiwi** are often active during the day.

Kākāpō

Active at night

Strigops habroptilus [Psittacidae]

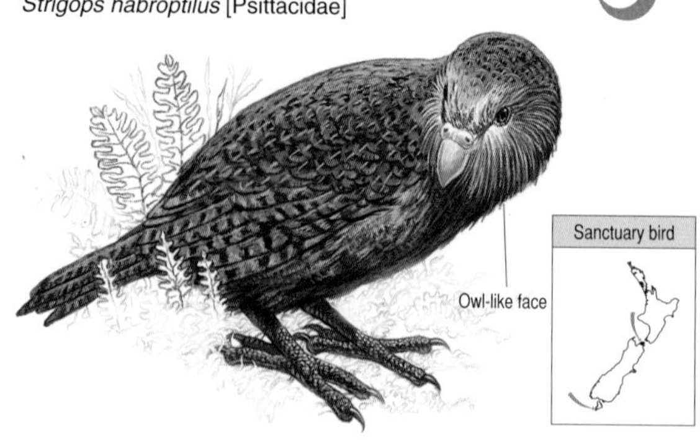

- ✓ **Only in native forest on Maud and Codfish Islands**
- ✓ Active mainly at night, when the male booms for hours
- ✓ Sweet-smelling
- ✓ Cannot fly

ENDEMIC

The world's heaviest parrot – weighing up to 3.4 kg. It is described as the native equivalent of the rabbit because of its strange diet and lifestyle, and is one of the world's rarest birds. Its Māori name ('night parrot') refers to the fact that it hides among rotting logs during the day and comes out only at night. Although a good runner and able to use its large wings to balance when climbing trees and vines, it cannot fly. The males gather in groups to make very loud booming sounds throughout most of the night. Nowadays, the bird is endangered, and found only in native forest on Maud and Codfish Islands. Neither of these islands are open to the public.

Takahē

Porphyrio hochstetteri [Rallidae]

- ✓ **Found naturally only in tussock grassland and beech forest west of Lake Te Anau**
- ✓ Stands almost knee-high (three times the bulk of a **pūkeko**)
- ✓ Cannot fly (unlike **pūkeko**, page 50)
- ✓ Call similar to **weka**: 'coo-eet'

ENDEMIC

Until its rediscovery in 1948, the takahē was thought to be extinct. Easily seen nowadays on Tiritiri Matangi and Kapiti Islands, also at Mt Bruce Wildlife Centre near Masterton and at Te Anau Wildlife Centre. This bird and the **pūkeko** are thought to be descended from the same bird: the **purple swamphen** of Australia. While the ancestors of the **pūkeko** appear to have arrived about 1000 years ago, it seems that the original ancestors of the takahē must have flown to New Zealand over ten million years ago, later gradually losing their ability to fly.

Index